BASEBALL

HUMOR

By
Charles S. Hellman and Robert A. Tiritilli

ISBN 0-935938-37-0
Illustrations by Robert A.Tiritilli
Cover & Interior Design by Charles S. Hellman
Edited by Charles S. Hellman

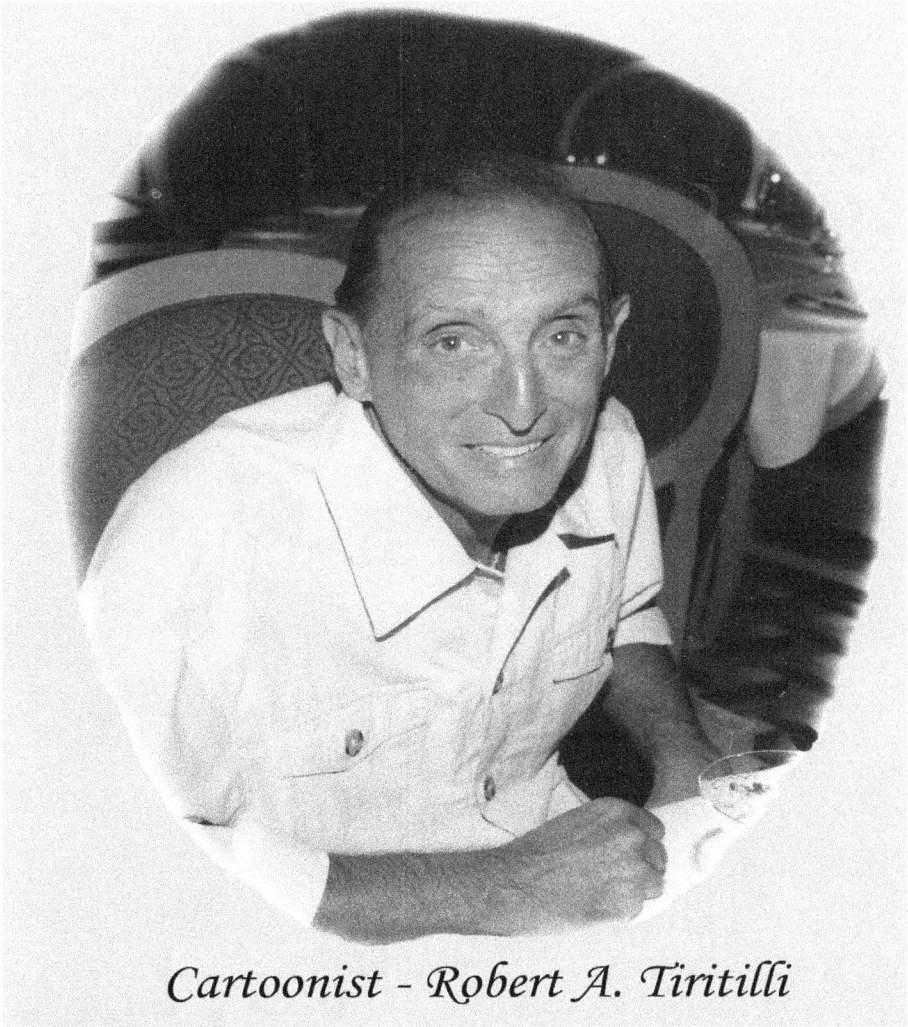

Cartoonist - Robert A. Tiritilli

With years of strong draftsman skills, Robert Tiritilli helped create his outlandish style and talent of sports cartooning by dually employing representative portraiture, and cartoonish lightheartedness.

Baseball Humor Review

There is a point in the life of every novice baseball fan when cartoons based on wordplay are hysterically funny. This humor book is for those who are at that joyous stage in life.

Baseball is defined as a bat-and-ball game played between two opposing teams who take turns batting and fielding. The game proceeds when a player on the fielding team, called the pitcher, throws a ball which a player on the batting team tries to hit with a bat. The objectives of the offensive team (batting team) are to hit the ball into the field of play, and to run the bases—having its runners advance counter-clockwise around four bases to score what are called "runs". The objective of the defensive team (fielding team) is to prevent batters from becoming runners, and to prevent runners' advance around the bases. A run is scored when a runner legally advances around the bases in order and touches home plate (the place where the player started as a batter). The team that scores the most runs by the end of the game is the winner.

Charles S. Hellman and Robert A. Tiritilli have clearly kept their ability to look at the world through ingenuous eyes, and we are the beneficiaries of their vision. You will feel many years younger as you recall the last time you saw the humor in "grownups" taking a sport too seriously.

The book contains over 100 one-paneled, pen and ink drawings that are reproduced in black and white except on the front and back cover of this soft cover book.

The front cover captures one of the better cartoons and gives you a sense of this book at its best . . . when it shifts the meaning of a baseball phrase into another one . . . but still within a baseball context. Play on words or images gives humor double meaning.

Some of the cartoons are not as clever as others. Can you imagine the one for "Bat"? Your guess won't be far off the mark. How about "Doubleheader"? The same applies. But in some cases, the cartoons take the obvious humor and make it better with a hilarious execution. "Bonus Baby" is a good example with a goofy looking youngster wearing a cap with a dollar sign on it while sitting in a baby buggy. This execution reminds you that paying a lot for a young ballplayer may not be the brightest idea in the world.

But almost all of these cartoons will tickle your funny bone. Youngsters, however, will have a few of the cartoons explained to them (as being a little more "adult" than their years such as "Pick Off " or employing baseball terms they may not know such as "Gopher Ball". From the youngster's point of view, this will be a four-star book because it doesn't have color inside.If your youngster is old enough to figure out the "Stealing Home Plate" cartoon without explanation, this book could be a good gift.

Baseball 101

"He can play any position he wants!"

Start of the *"BAMBINO CURSE"*

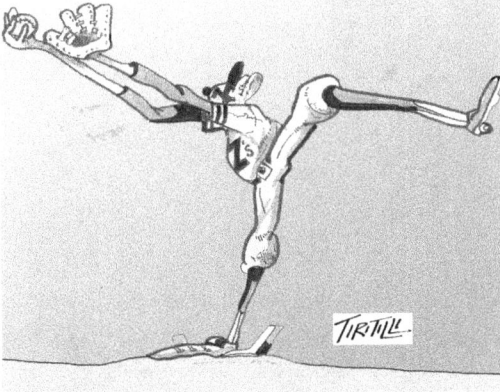

Into the stretch

Types of PITCHERS

Warming up   **Pick-off**

"Here we go! *CUBS... CLIPPERS... ARIZONA... FLORIDA...*

"Remember... don't sit between us!"

Yogi quoting Shakespeare...

Mother's Day at Yankee Stadium

First night game at Wrigley Field

Changeup

Knuckle ball

Types of BASEBALLS

Gopher ball

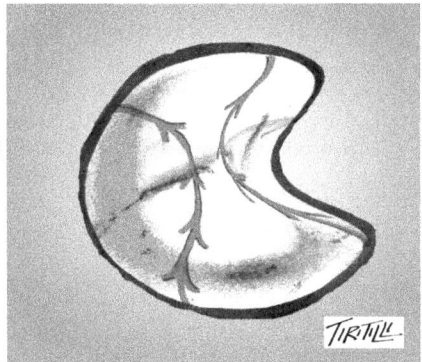

Curve ball

In-field fly ball

Abner Doubleday switches from sapphire to diamond baseball field.

17

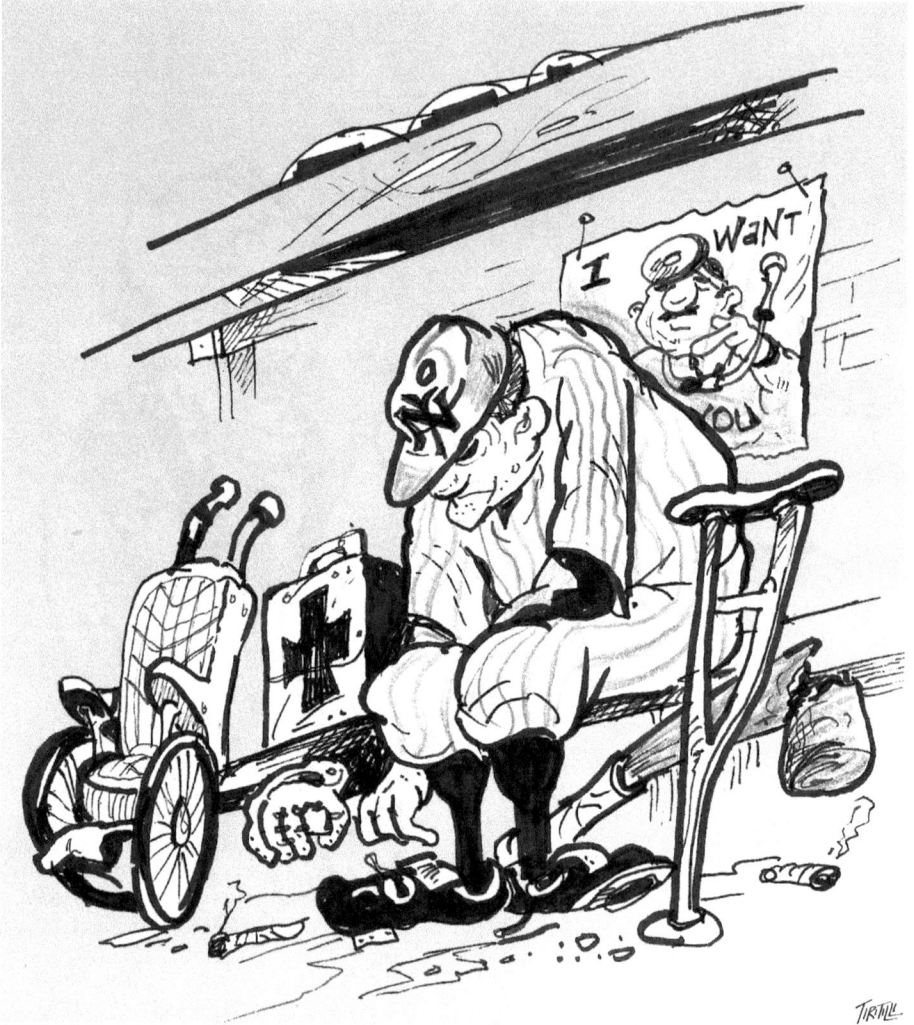

Steroids... NOT worth it!

**Dr. Quack attempts to clone the Babe...
ends up with a candy bar!**

Babe Ruth points to catcher...
promptly strikes out!

20

Advanced scout

Vendor

3rd baseman's cannon arm

Bring in the fireman

Types of PLAYERS

Banjo hitter

Bonus baby

Double header

**"Someone told them
I was a baseball scout!"**

**Manager mixes-up...
Bottom of the Fifth!**

**Coach Casey won't let
GOOD ENOUGH alone.**

Beer here!

"What part of
STRIKE THREE
don't you understand?"

Ump-eye-er

Types of Umpires

"Where's the umpire Umpire Burnout
when you need him?"

Liner to center field

Mayor of Detroit lays cornerstone for new stadium that entombs Jimmy Hoffa.

**"Who wants
HAPPY HOUR to start early?"**

**Drugs, lies, cheating...
I just love the playoffs!**

"You have a BASEBALL theory, huh?"

Since GOD started calling plays for the Angels, they haven't lost a game!

"Baseball News is NOT Fake news!

"I don't write FAKE News!

Steroids have made Buster so huge he needs air bags. In addition he can be seen circling the moon!

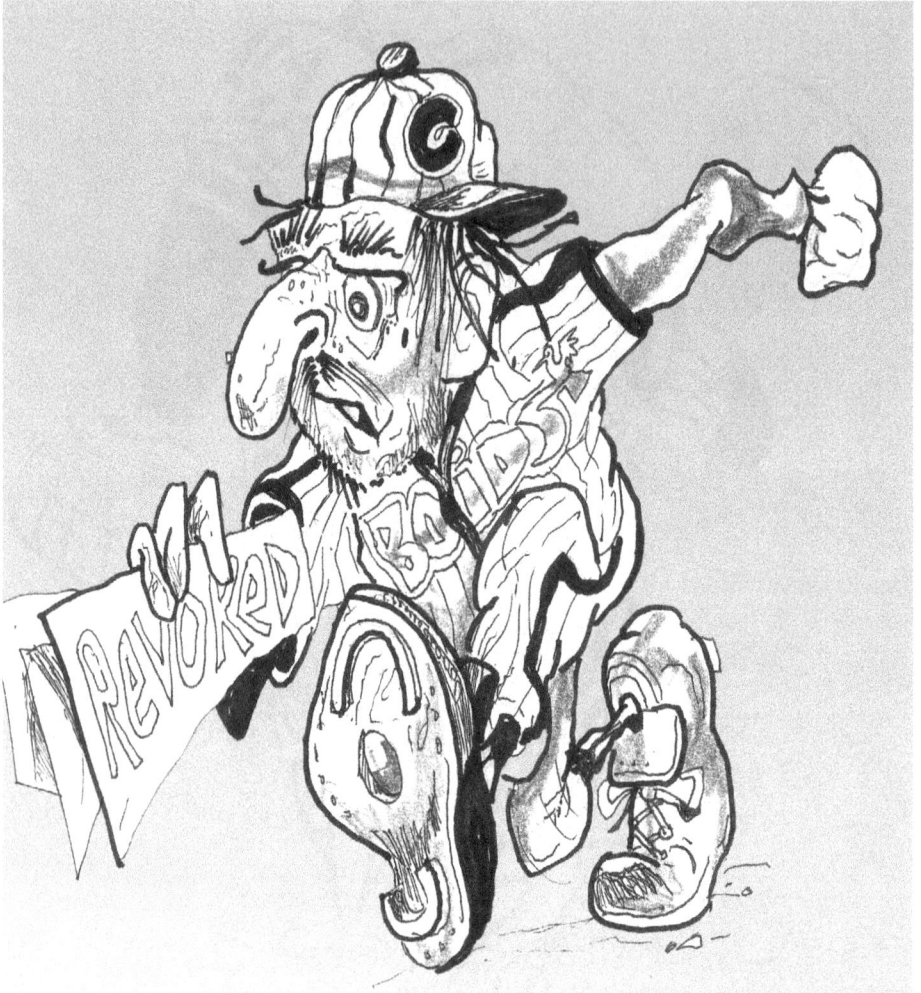

**The Commissioner "REVOKES"
Casey's license to steal!**

After 321 ejections -
Homer at the Pearly Gates!

Ball Boy

Curve ball

Types of BASEBALLS

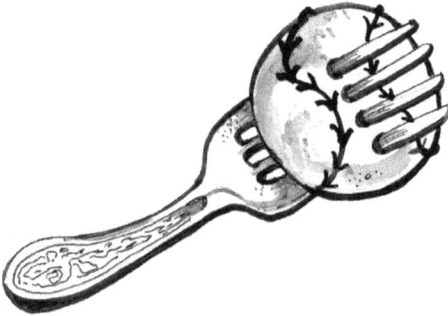

Fork ball

Base-on-balls

Chernobyl Youth Baseball League

"It's the biggest baseball contract yet!"

**"There!
That should clear up a few things!**

Einstein was a major league prospect until he discovered "The Law of Gravity".

Slugger hasn't missed a ball all summer.

"There he goes again...
flying off the handle."

**Coach Munger says,
"In my days, that would never happen!"**

Box Seats...
Ground level   **Sky Box**

Types of SEATS

Cheap seats

**A Cleveland Indian encounters
the first dreaded "Infield Fly"!**

Pop up

Caught in a PICKLE

Giving signals

Good hands

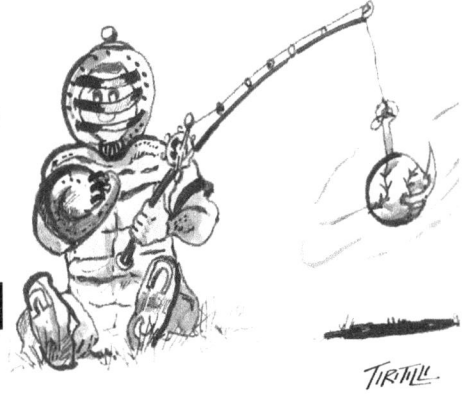
Catcher

Types of PLAYERS

Long ball hitter

Moog accidently becomes
first FIREBALLER

Shoeless "Joe" Jackson gets cold feet!

In the batter's box

"I can play better with my eyes shut!"

Fowl Ball

Goof ball

Types of BASEBALLS

Fly Ball

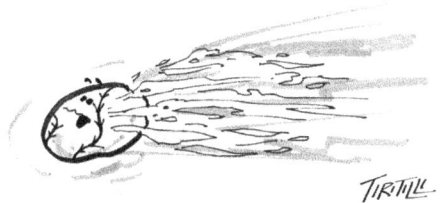
Fireball

**"Get up!
The game is NOT over, yet!"**

Call 911

Outstanding in his field

Another "Whistleblower" player leaves the game and joins the Federal Witness Protection Program!

Lauching pad

Bat

Money player

"Pinch" hitter

Types of PLAYERS

Catcher

Slugger

Drag bunt

Sacrifice

Foul line

Digging in to the batter's box

TIRTILL

Scoreboard

Don't eat the bat donut

ShowBoat

Bring in the fireman

Types of PLAYERS

Base stealer

Superstitious Player

Error

Hook slide

Batting helmets

Pennant drive

Sliide

Hitter's park

Pitcher's park

Spitball

Base-ball

Types of BASEBALLS

Screwball

Sinker

On the bag

Fan

Rubber armed

Glass arm

Types of PITCHERS

Wild pitcher

Gotta gun for an arm

Three-bagger

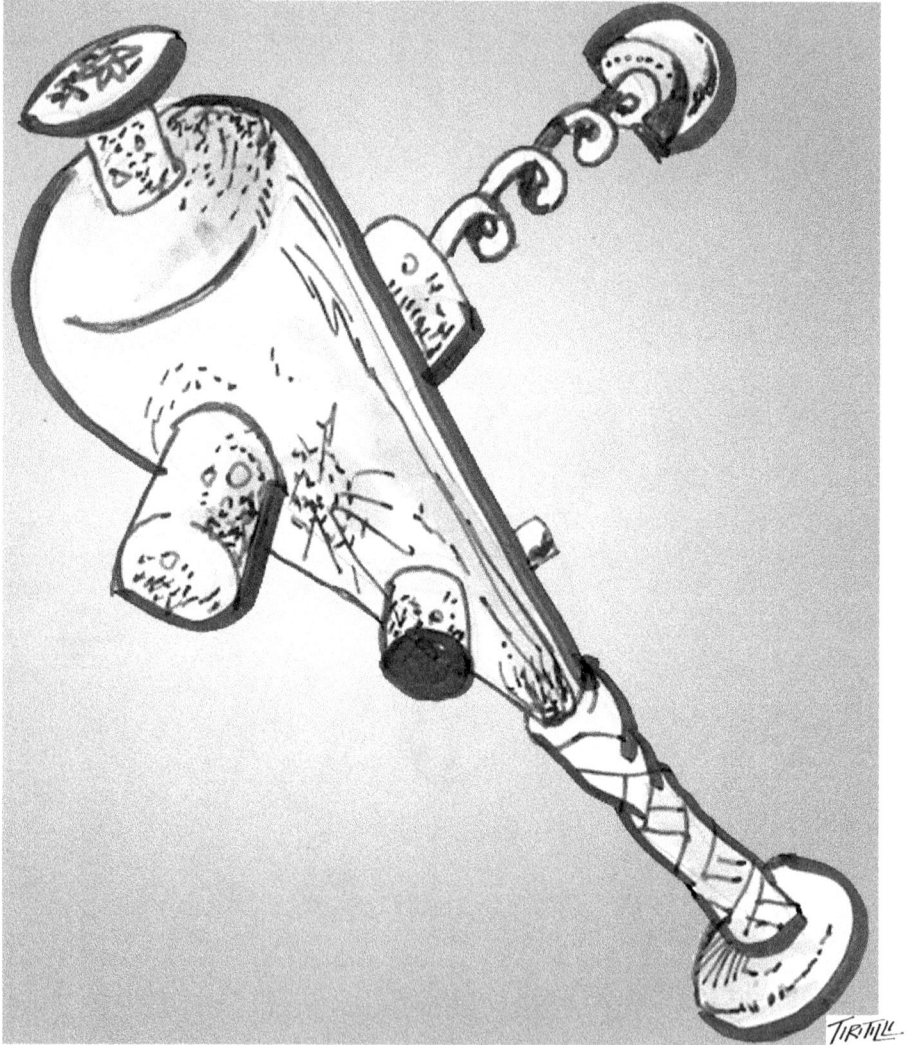

Corked?

"You have a rifle arm,
but its the wrong caliber!"

"Professor, baseball players don't understand QUANTUM PHYSICS!"

Sold drugs to Little Leaguers

Michaelangelo creates "GOD".
GOD creates Baseball.

Munkus refuses to bat last.

"Rocky" is a face baseball!

**Queen Mother celebrates her
200th birthday...
throws out first pitch at Yankee Stadium.**

Lots of finger pointing at the Sport's Negotiation Committee Meeting

"Lefty, I hear you're a good glove man!"

**"You can tell he was a ...
Baseball Player!"**

**"Those fans know how to
PUSH YOUR BUTTONS!"**

**BABE comes through...
ends up in Hog Heaven!**

Baseball Owner gambling

"You said we should
"*TOUCH BASE*" sometime."

**"I dub you *Sir Loin*,
well done!"**

"The boys haven't forgotten about you. They keep asking... *Where is Stinky?"*

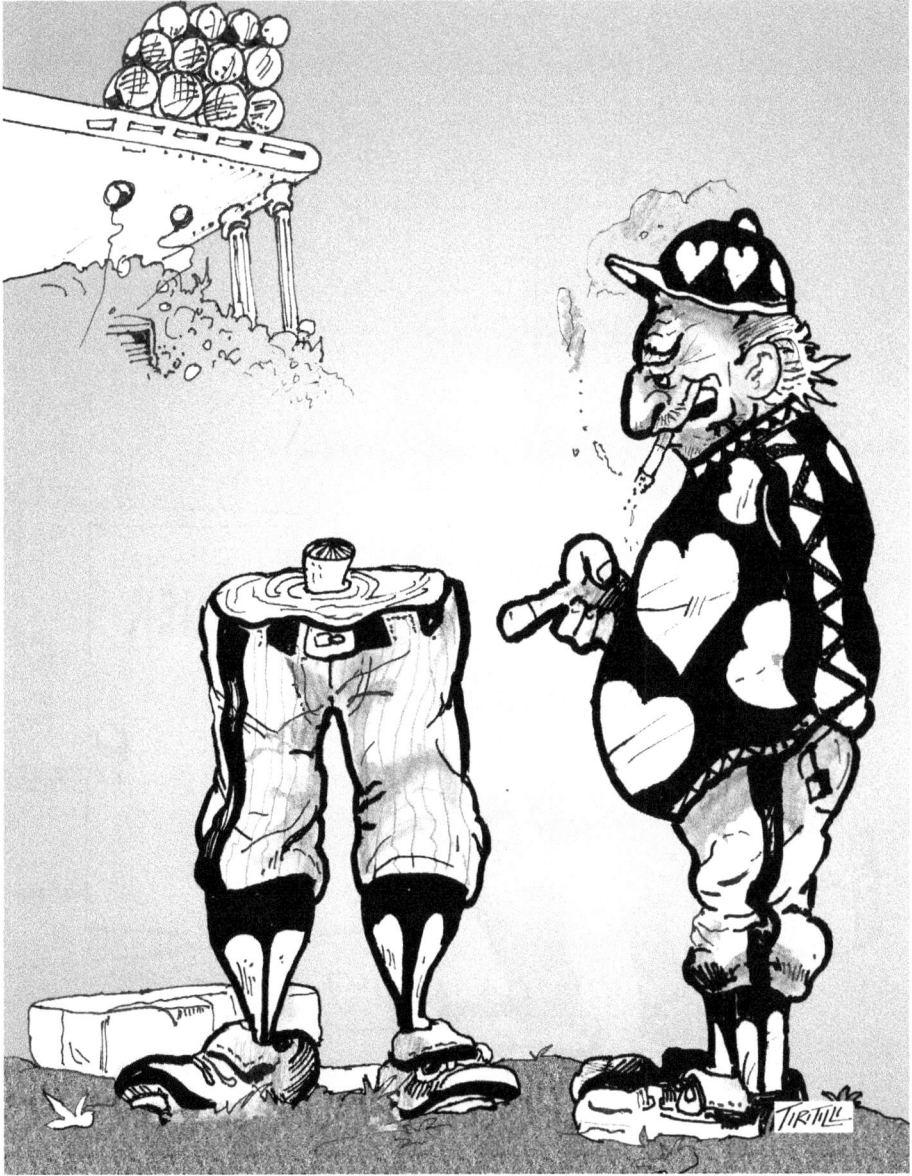

**"AH! Ha! The perfect
CUT-OFF man!"**

"Too bad you're late. He tore up your
baseball contract a minute ago."

**Baseball fans must learn
to think outside the box!**

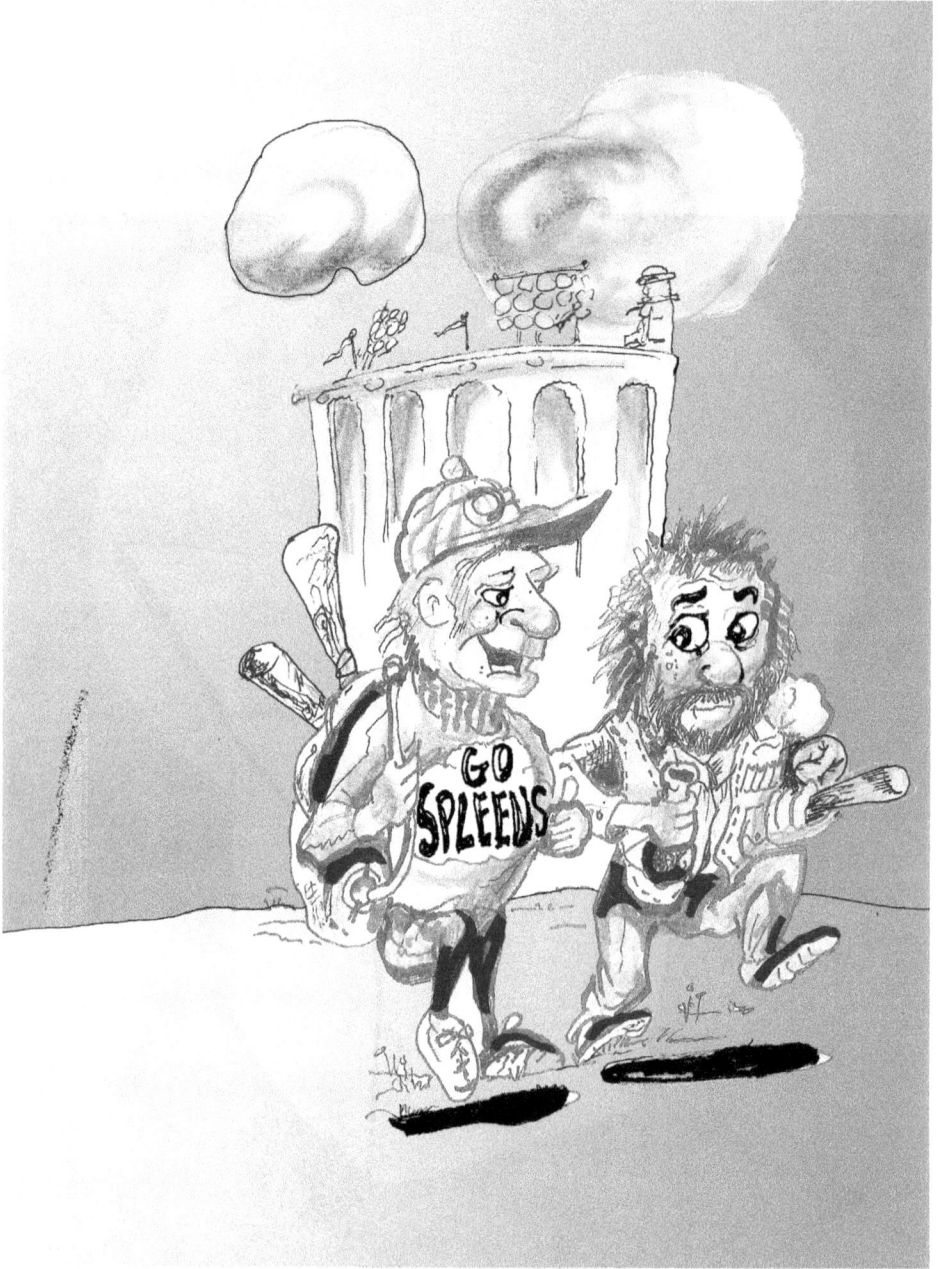

**"I don't think you're quite
ready for the majors!"**

"Maybe *less* exercise will help your batting average!"

"You want me to be an umpire?"

"Who wants to go to the World Series?"

Sport Education

**"I traded our box seats
for a week in Arizona."**

"I'm a full blooded Indian, what percent of Indian blood do you have?"

"A chicken mascot gets no respect!"

Fan's fan!

Millenniums ??

**"Sorry... take it back.
Our mantle isn't large enough."**

"Who said money isn't a motivator?"

**"Motivation, HELL!
It just puts them to sleep."**

"He's got WiFi."

The baseball's first cell phone call.

**"Rise your hand
if you were a baseball umpire."**

"My fastball once was clocked
over 110mph!"

"Sorry, I've never heard of
Abbott and Costello!"

"Who's on first?"

"What's on second!"

"Don't Know's on third!"

"Honey, they want me
to be a pinch hitter!"

Fritz proved that the game of baseball is our national pastime.

"Don't fret! You're just like Einstein.
He got D's in college. He also got F's."

**"I'm going to graduate on time
NO matter how long it takes!"**

"I start exercising at six o'clock in the morning NO MATTER what time is."

"I'm not perfect,
but I'm perfect for your baseball team."

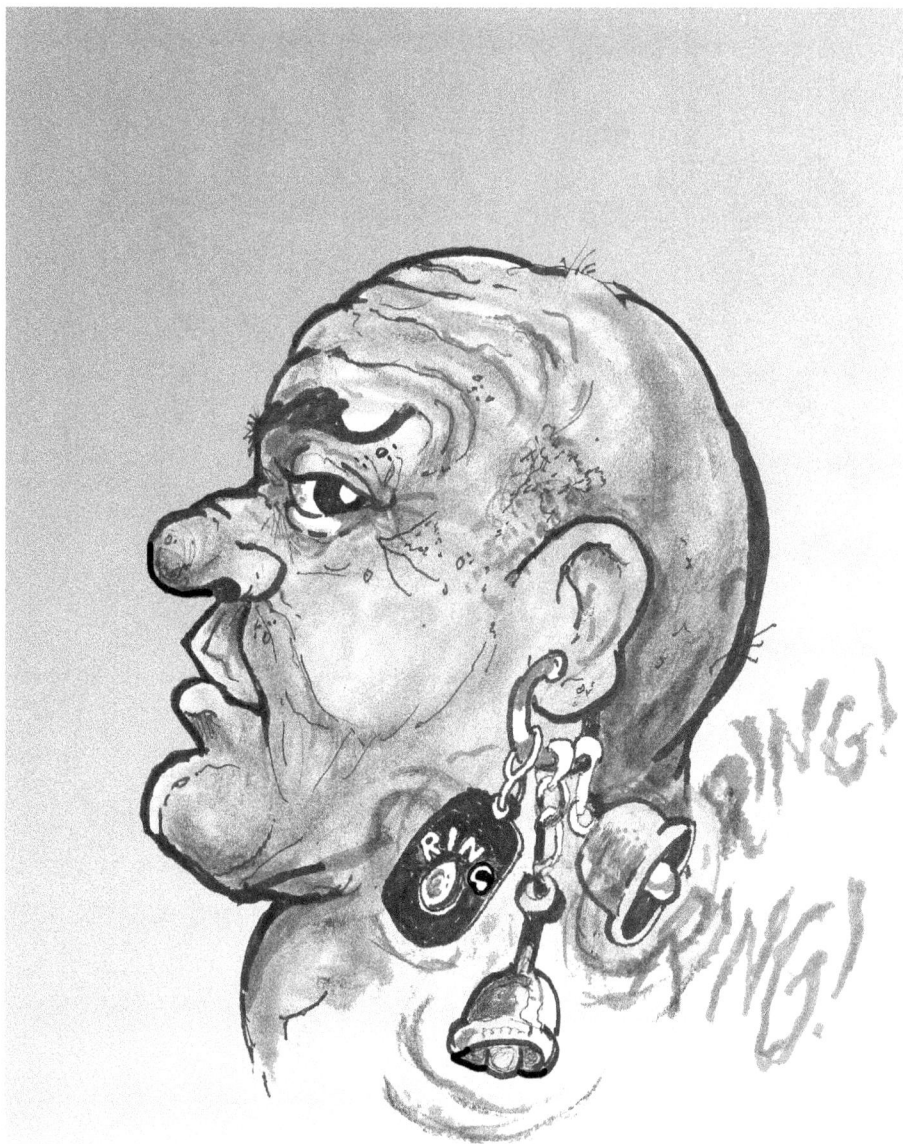

Real baseball players wear earRINGS!

"I promote those players
from the minors to the majors
because they've been there a while."

"It take a lot of team violence
to finally get him to smile!"

**"Big Foot" meets "Big Foot"
before their EPIC baseball game!**

"There is no "EYE" in team!"

**"Raise your hand,
if you were on the baseball team last year."**

"You can play baseball or checkers!"

"I always keep a picture of my agent on my locker so I can fine my clothes!"

"I used to play for the Reindeer's baseball team!"

Mr. Sports!

"Nobody in baseball
should be considered a genius.
A genius is a guy like Ezra Einstein!"

FREE HOTDOGS!

**Baseball losers are doomed
to the rath of HELL's BELLS!**

"You got this from coaching a Little League team, huh?"

"I never thought I'd get jail time
for stealing home plate."

"So you played three years at SING-SING.
That doesn't strike a cord with me!"

Robert A. Tiritilli

Award-winning cartoonist, Robert A. Tiritilli—a true sports aficionado—is passionate about all sports and loves to make fun of the pastime and all those who play it. He has drawn 1,000's of different sports cartoons and creates his outlandish style of sports cartooning by combining representative portraiture with cartoonish light-heartedness.

He uses a unique sense of silliness to strike a chord with anyone who plays or enjoys sports, whether they are athletes or couch potatoes.

He finds more ways to blend humorous cartoons with crafty captions. This cartoonist plays with a deck of cards containing every shade of sports humor—wit, satire, jesting, and clowning.

Laugh until your sides hurt with his collections of hilarious sports cartoons! Tiritilli has put the "F" back into the word "FUN."

Sports has more words, terms, and phrases that lend themselves to humorous reinterpretation based on their literal meaning.

The fun of these cartoons at its best is when it shifts the meaning of a sports phrase into another one. But in some cases, the pictures take the obvious joke and make it better with a hilarious execution.

www.ingramcontent.com/pod-product-compliance
Lightning Source LLC
Chambersburg PA
CBHW061728020426
42331CB00006B/1147